Cornerstones of Freedom

The Natchez Trace

LINDA AND CHARLES GEORGE

CHILDREN'S PRESS®
A Division of Scholastic Inc.
New York • Toronto • London • Auckland • Sydney
Mexico City • New Delhi • Hong Kong
Danbury, Connecticut

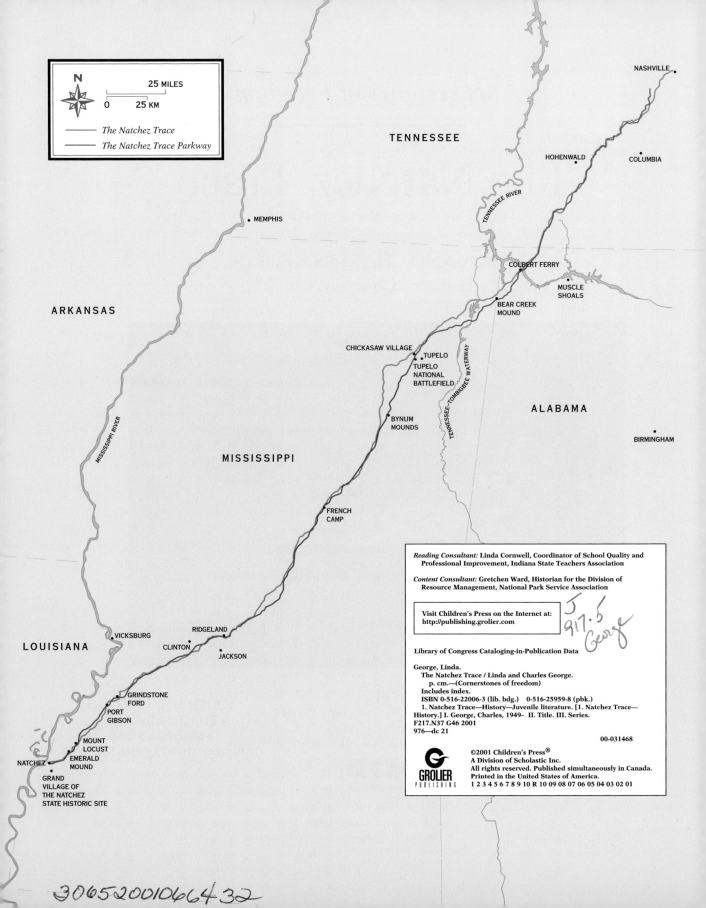

Reading Consultant: Linda Cornwell, Coordinator of School Quality and Professional Improvement, Indiana State Teachers Association

Content Consultant: Gretchen Ward, Historian for the Division of Resource Management, National Park Service Association

Visit Children's Press on the Internet at:
http://publishing.grolier.com

Library of Congress Cataloging-in-Publication Data

George, Linda.
   The Natchez Trace / Linda and Charles George.
      p. cm.—(Cornerstones of freedom)
   Includes index.
   ISBN 0-516-22006-3 (lib. bdg.)   0-516-25959-8 (pbk.)
   1. Natchez Trace—History—Juvenile literature. [1. Natchez Trace—History.] I. George, Charles, 1949– II. Title. III. Series.
F217.N37 G46 2001
976—dc 21

                                                    00-031468

For countless centuries, herds of bison and deer traveled from winter to summer grazing areas along a route that would become known as the Natchez Trace. (Trace is another word for trail.) Members of the Choctaw, Chickasaw, and Natchez tribes followed the same route, going from village to village. As early as the mid-1700s, the same narrow trail—through present-day Tennessee, Alabama, and Mississippi—provided a pathway for explorers, shopkeepers, and pioneers. After they transported goods down the Ohio and Mississippi Rivers to Natchez, Mississippi, they sold their goods and their flatboats. Then they headed northeast on the well-worn path.

The name of the trail from Natchez, Mississippi, to Nashville, Tennessee, changed through the years. In the late 1700s, people had three different names for the trail—"the Path to the Choctaw Nation," "The Choctaw–Chickasaw Trail," and "The Chickasaw Trace." By the early 1800s, travelers called the route "The Natchez Road" or "The Nashville Road," depending on which way they were going. In 1826, the entire path became known as "The Natchez Trace."

Most trails that connected the United States to its frontiers were west of the Mississippi River. People traveled from Missouri to New Mexico along The Santa Fe Trail. The Oregon Trail went from Missouri to Oregon. The Natchez Trace is east of the Mississippi. The Trace connected the United States with its newly acquired frontier along the lower Mississippi River. In the late 1700s and early 1800s, this region was considered the Southwest—what is now Mississippi, Louisiana, Alabama, Arkansas, and eastern Texas. Without the Natchez Trace, the United States could have lost control of trade in the Southwest.

The history of the Natchez Trace stretches back to a time before people lived in the southern forests of North America. For centuries, grazing animals made their way through the lush lower Mississippi region. They created a path by crossing creeks and skirting swamps and rocky ravines. Scientists say ancient American Indian tribes reached the area about 12,000 years ago. Over the centuries, their ancestors trekked the animal trails, followed the high ground, and avoided the low-lying wetlands. Ancient tribes constructed huge earthen mounds near these animal trails. Historians think these mounds were ceremonial centers or burial places.

The first Europeans walked the Natchez Trace in 1540. Spanish explorer Hernando de Soto and his expedition crossed the Trace in present-day Mississippi. They spent the winter of 1540–1541 near the trail. They eventually traveled through much of what is now the southeastern United States.

This illustration shows Hernando de Soto, members of his expedition, and American Indians on the shore of the Mississippi River.

More than a century later, French explorers floated down the Mississippi River. Father Jacques Marquette and trapper Louis Joliet landed near the Natchez Trace in 1673. Nine years later, they were followed by René-Robert Cavelier, Sieur de La Salle. La Salle claimed for France the land along the Mississippi River. He thought the French should build forts along the river to defend their land.

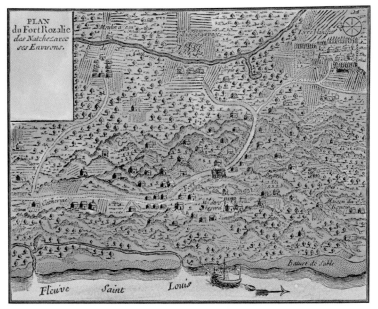

A mapmaker drew this map of Fort Rosalie in 1770.

In 1716, the French established Fort Rosalie at the site of present-day Natchez, Mississippi. This fort was the first European settlement near the Natchez Trace. The Grand Village of the Natchez, the center of activity for the Natchez Indians, was near the fort. As early as 1733, the French mapped an Indian trail extending from the Grand Village toward the Northeast. Arguments between the French and the Natchez led to bloodshed. By 1743, the tribe had been wiped out, but a settlement near Fort Rosalie took the tribe's name.

The town of Natchez became an important river port because of its location on the Mississippi. Four nations fought to control the port. The

French ruled Natchez first, then the Spanish, then the British. The residents of Natchez rode the changing tides of leadership. Political control of much of the area along the Natchez Trace

passed to the newly formed United States in 1783 after its victory over Great Britain in the Revolutionary War. On April 7, 1798, the U.S. Congress established the Mississippi Territory. Natchez became the new territory's capital.

Natchez, Mississippi, became an important center for trade because of its location on the banks of the Mississippi River.

In August 1798, U.S. President John Adams sent Winthrop Sargent to serve as the Mississippi Territory's first governor. Two events contributed to the success of the Mississippi Territory. In 1801, Sargent asked the Choctaw and Chickasaw tribes for permission for the U.S. Army to build a road through their lands. The road would follow the long-used American Indian trail and would link Natchez and Nashville, Tennessee. Two years later, the United States purchased the Louisiana Territory from France. The size of the United States nearly doubled. The Louisiana Purchase also gave American traders the right to sail the Mississippi River for free.

This 1775 drawing shows a Choctaw Indian.

The Mississippi River and the Natchez Trace were important to trade. Families who lived in the Ohio River valley began floating their goods downriver to the Mississippi, and on to New Orleans. As this custom increased, people needed an overland route by which they could return home. With such a route, trade would thrive because people in the central United States could sell their goods in the lower Mississippi region.

The series of trails stretching from Natchez to Nashville, through lands controlled by the Choctaw and Chickasaw, provided the needed route. However, the Natchez Trace was difficult to travel. Most of the trail was so narrow that people and horses had to walk single file. The land along the Trace—sucking swamps, rocky ground, swift creeks, and mile-wide rivers—prevented travelers from widening the path. It took nearly a month to make the almost 450-mile (724-kilometer) trip from Natchez to Nashville. Without a great deal of luck and help from American Indians along the way, many travelers would not have survived the trip.

One such traveler was Francis Baily. On July 4, 1797, Baily left Natchez for Nashville along the narrow Natchez Trace. In his journal, he recorded his party's difficult journey. Their journey was typical of most travelers on the Trace. Before setting foot on the trail, the

Francis Baily

party of thirteen gathered food for what they believed would be a three-week trip. They killed an ox and dried the meat. They baked 25 pounds (11 kilograms) of hard biscuit. For each person, they packed 6 pounds (3 kg) of flour, 12 pounds (5 kg) of bacon, 3 pounds (1 kg) of rice, some coffee, and some sugar. Each person also took a small bag of cornmeal to eat in case food supplies ran out. A spoonful of cornmeal with some water swelled in a person's stomach,

This heavily wooded section of the Natchez Trace is near Grindstone Ford.

staving off hunger during lean times. Thirty horses would help carry the supplies.

For about 60 miles (96 km), "The Path to the Choctaw Nation" was a long but uneventful walk for Baily and his companions. At Grindstone Ford, near present-day Port Gibson, Mississippi, they crossed the shallow water of Bayou Pierre. Here, the Natchez Trace became wild country. Before long, they were in danger.

Members of the party crossed creeks too deep to ford by walking across fallen trees spanning the steep banks. Step by step, they carefully carried precious supplies across while their horses swam. Some sections of the trail were barely visible. Numerous smaller paths branched out from the Natchez Trace, but fallen trees and branches or dense underbrush often hid these paths. Without help from the Choctaw and Chickasaw tribes, Baily and his companions might have become hopelessly lost.

The group's daily routine provided some comfort. Their routine consisted of packing the horses, traveling until mid-day or until they found water, then unpacking the horses for two or three hours of rest. Then they repeated the routine.

Water was often scarce. Several times, Baily "shouted for joy" when they came across "a nasty, dirty puddle." Drinking such polluted water often led to illness, and Baily was forced to leave sick people behind. Although Baily and the healthy members would travel on, they sent Chickasaw from the next village to help the sick.

Sometime around July 20, 1797, Baily and his companions arrived at Bigtown. This Chickasaw village had several clusters of four or five huts, and it was near present-day Tupelo, Mississippi. Villagers grew corn and vegetables and tended apple and peach orchards. Smaller villages were

nearby. Upon entering the village, the Chickasaw surrounded the travelers and offered them chances to swap, or trade. The Chickasaw had learned this word from earlier travelers. Baily declined to swap his hat, even after repeated offers.

From Bigtown, the Baily party walked up hills and crossed branches of the Tombigbee River. Here, they accidentally walked through poison ivy. They called it "poison vine." Their legs itched and swelled from exposure to the plant. They had to slit their trouser legs and cut the tops off their boots to make room for their swollen legs. With itchy, swollen legs, they continued walking.

Signs mark the foundation of a preserved Chickasaw village on the Natchez Trace. The remnants of the foundation show the layout of the village.

Baily and his companions had been on the trail nearly three weeks when they had to cross the mile-wide Tennessee River. Forced to cut wood and build rafts, Baily was almost swept away by the swift current while clinging to a raft loaded with supplies. Friendly Cherokees rescued Baily and his party. The Cherokees shared a meal with the weary travelers. Then the party lugged supplies 20 feet (6 meters) up the steep, slippery riverbank, just west of present-day Muscle Shoals, Alabama.

The Tennessee River

The tired but determined group was 125 miles (201 km) from Nashville when a person they met on the trail told them another local tribe, the Creek, was on the warpath. Baily and his party did not want the Creek to see or hear them. They slept without fires and whispered. They lived on a spoonful of cornmeal a day because they had eaten the rest of their food.

Days later, the hungry travelers finally ate a meal. They encountered two Chickasaws they had met earlier. The Chickasaws fed them roasted venison, or deer meat, dipped in honey. Baily exclaimed, "No meal was ever so grateful as this." Given enough venison for the remainder of the trip, Baily and his party pushed on. They went to Duck River and Lick Creek, west of present-day Columbia, Tennessee. Bison had come there for hundreds of years to lick salt. Twenty-seven days after leaving Natchez, they sighted Nashville on the morning of July 31, 1797. Baily wrote, "The sight of it gave us great pleasure."

Deer roam a section of the Natchez Trace in Alabama.

Baily would have been delighted to have a place to stay along the Natchez Trace. In the early 1800s, people established homes, supply depots, and stands along the treacherous pathway between Natchez and Nashville. Most stands were little more than shacks where people could eat and rest, yet they were a welcome sight to tired travelers. The smaller

Mount Locust is the only restored stand remaining along the Natchez Trace.

stands usually served greasy food and provided a soggy, insect-infested cot, but most people preferred staying at a stand to eating nothing and sleeping on the ground.

Between 1800 and 1820, more than twenty stands were built along the Natchez Trace. Among the best known of these crude establishments was Doak's Stand. Later, this stand became a stagecoach stop. Another well-known stand was French Camp. A Frenchman named Louis Le Fleur opened this stand in 1810. Of all the stands along the trail, only Mount Locust and Red Bluff were large enough to be called inns.

Stands offered little relief from the dangers of the trail. Travelers were often robbed while sleeping in stands. Many people buried their valuables before entering a stand, and they either took turns sleeping or slept with their guns at the ready.

Between stands, travelers sometimes trudged through swamps or had to contend with terrible weather. When people or horses became stuck in a swamp, they found it difficult to escape. Travelers often braved torrential rains or winds from Gulf of Mexico hurricanes. Sometimes floods stopped travelers along the Natchez Trace. After swamps, storms, or floods, even the most meager stand was a welcome sight.

The biggest fear of most people who traveled the Natchez Trace, however, was being robbed. Greedy and ruthless thieves stole money from honest folks on their way to Nashville. Strung out single file in the dark woods, travelers were easy prey for bandits and murderers. Some of the worst of these villains were Joseph Thompson Hare, the Mason gang, and the cruel and vicious Harpe Brothers.

Thieves prepare to rob a stagecoach on the Natchez Trace.

Joseph Thompson Hare, called a hoodlum by most historians, was educated and religious—but ruthless. Hare and his fellow outlaws dressed and painted their faces "like Indians on the warpath" so that others would suspect the Choctaw and Chickasaw. He grew rich on stolen doubloons (gold Spanish coins), gold bars, and silver dollars taken from unlucky travelers. Hare murdered a number of people on the Natchez Trace during the early 1800s. He was hanged in Maryland for robbing a night mail coach.

In 1801, another group of outlaws—Samuel Mason and his gang—began robbing travelers on the Natchez Trace. Law officers caught Mason and his son and accused them of robbing Colonel Joshua Baker of a large sum of money. Mason and his son were sentenced to thirty-nine lashes and branded. They were also locked into pillories, wooden devices with holes for prisoners' heads and hands. Pillories were not tall enough for prisoners to stand erect, causing them terrible pain in the back and legs. One reporter wrote that Mason and his son's ears were nailed to the pillories and then cut off. After they endured this punishment for a crime they insisted they did not commit, Mason and his gang turned really mean. Instead of robbing their victims, they began murdering them.

In 1803, a $2,000 reward was offered for Mason—dead or alive. Two men in his gang, James Mays and John Setton, attacked Mason with a tomahawk while he slept. They cut off his head, packed it in blue clay to preserve it, and presented their trophy to the authorities.

A law officer whips a criminal tied to a whipping post. Above them, a prisoner stands in a pillory.

Setton, one of the men who murdered Mason, was one of the Harpe Brothers. They were the most evil outlaws on The Natchez Trace. Headed by "Big Harpe" (Micajah Harpe) and "Little Harpe" (Wiley Harpe), the gang struck fear even in the hearts of other bandits and murderers. The Harpe Brothers came to the Trace from North Carolina before 1800, and they frightened people from the Tennessee valley to the Natchez bluffs. They tortured and killed their victims. Their favorite method of torture included slitting their victim's abdomen, removing its contents, and filling the cavity with rocks. When the victim was dead, they threw the body into a river or creek. They killed women and children as easily as they killed men. Big Harpe once killed his own baby to stop its crying.

This illustration shows a vigilante committee breaking into a man's home and accusing him of a crime.

A vigilante committee— people banded together to find and capture outlaws—finally seized Big Harpe after he killed a woman and her child. The woman's husband witnessed the murder of his

18

wife and child, and he wanted revenge. He was allowed to slowly sever Big Harpe's head. Then he stuck it in the fork of a tree.

Many people who managed to survive a journey on the Natchez Trace called it "The Devil's Backbone." No one knows the origin of this name, but the reference to the devil probably comes from the hardships, dangers, and evil villains that people encountered on the trail. In spite of these difficulties, thousands of people traveled the Trace. In places, the pathway sank from constant use. Some sections sank as much as 20 feet (6 m) lower than the surrounding ground.

This photograph shows a section of the sunken Trace. The soft, fine soils in the lower Mississippi region cannot withstand heavy use.

Timothy Pickering

Improvements to the road began in 1801, thanks in part to the urging of Andrew Jackson. He had traveled the Natchez Trace with his wife, Rachel, after their marriage in Natchez in 1791. Many people realized that the Trace was an important communication link between the Northeast and the Southwest. Letters or government dispatches took longer to travel from Philadelphia to Natchez than they took to travel from Philadelphia to Europe. U.S. Secretary of State Timothy Pickering, along with the Postmaster General, proposed using the Trace as a postal route between the United States and its southwestern frontier.

Early in 1800, a man named Abijah Hunt received a contract to carry the mail between Nashville and Natchez. In April, Congress designated the Natchez Trace a post road. People began plans for building the road. Between 1801 and 1809, federal troops under the direction of General James Wilkinson cut trees and underbrush. They widened the narrow path. They bridged some of the creeks and rivers it crossed and built causeways, or raised roadways, through its swamps.

One of the first post riders on the Natchez Trace was John L. Swaney. In 1800, his round-trip trek took about one month. The mail sack he carried was "a deerskin pouch well treated with oil to prevent water from ruining its contents." He usually delivered newspapers, a few personal letters, and government dispatches to the territorial governor.

This illustration shows a post rider carrying the mail.

The regular postal schedule eventually called for one post rider to leave Nashville every second Sunday at 9:00 A.M. while another left Natchez at the same time. The riders met at Hoolky Creek, just south of present-day Tupelo, near the property of John McIntosh. After exchanging mail and resting a day, the riders retraced their steps.

Other regulars on the Natchez Trace were traveling preachers. The most unusual of these preachers was Lorenzo Dow. Since childhood, Dow felt he had been chosen by God to preach. He preached to anyone who would listen— and sometimes to those who did not want to listen! He sometimes lured people to a church, then bolted the door and stood against it. He refused to let the crowd leave until he delivered his fiery but scary message. Sometimes they became angry with him.

Lorenzo Dow

Tall and thin, with pale skin, Dow never cut his hair. His beard tangled into "a red-brown maze," while the hair on his head hung below his shoulders. His clothing hung in tatters. People described him as "a bunch of hair on a sorry nag." He continued his ministry by begging for bread from people he met. He traded his only possession—a watch—for a piece of land in the Kingston settlement, near Natchez. He established a church there in 1803.

The Kingston United Methodist Church was organized in 1800. Three years later, Lorenzo Dow bought a lot near this church.

Stories of people who traveled the Natchez Trace are numerous. Although each story is slightly different, there were two common traits among the travelers on the Trace. They had a determination to find prosperity in what had once been wilderness, and they wanted to bring their culture to the southwestern frontier of the United States. The Trace continued to bring new people and changes to the lower Mississippi region until 1812. That year, a new invention led to the famous pathway becoming obsolete.

The Delta Queen *(left) and the* Mississippi Queen *(right) are modeled after steamboats that navigated the Mississippi River in the 1800s.*

That invention was the steam engine. In January 1812, the steamboat *New Orleans* arrived in Natchez. Many more steamboats followed in the years to come. Before the invention of the steamboat, it was difficult to move upstream—against the current—on the Mississippi. Steamboats could travel north on the Mississippi River, then northeast on the Ohio. They provided people who had floated their goods downriver to Natchez and New Orleans with an easier, faster, and safer way to return to the Northeast.

The Natchez Trace was no longer necessary to link the nation together. The people who lived along the trail built better roads. Brush, trees, and tall grass gradually recaptured much of the route. For a long time, all that remained of the Trace were small stretches used locally and the recollections of old-timers who remembered its heyday.

In the 1930s, The Natchez Trace was resurrected as part of President Franklin D. Roosevelt's program to create more jobs during the Great Depression. In 1934, the National Park Service began a project that continues today—the construction of a parkway, a scenic highway, from Natchez to Nashville. Advertising billboards, commercial vehicles, and businesses are forbidden along the parkway. The speed limit, a leisurely 50 miles (80 km) per hour, allows travelers to relax and enjoy the view.

This section of the Natchez Trace Parkway is in Tennessee.

Along the 443-mile (713-km) parkway, markers detail important historical sites from Nashville to Natchez. A section of the old Trace, just southwest of Nashville, marks where the U.S. Army cleared a section of "The Natchez Road" in 1801. Farther to the southwest, near Hohenwald, Tennessee, is the grave of Meriwether Lewis. In 1809, the leader of the Lewis and Clark Expedition died mysteriously of gunshot wounds while traveling to Washington, D.C.

Once visitors cross the Tennessee border into Alabama, they can see Colbert Ferry, on the Tennessee River. Here, George Colbert reportedly charged part of Andrew Jackson's Tennessee army $75,000 to transport them across the river. The army was on its way to fight the Battle of New Orleans, an important battle in the War of 1812. War touched the Natchez Trace again. The site of the 1864 Civil War battle, Tupelo National Battlefield, is in the city of Tupelo, Mississippi—just east of the Natchez Trace Parkway.

Near the Tupelo National Battlefield, the preserved site of a Chickasaw village records the early history and daily life of the tribe. American Indians play an important role in the history of the Natchez Trace. Numerous Indian mounds dating back to prehistoric times are scattered along the parkway. These sites include Bynum Mounds, southwest of Tupelo, and Emerald Mound, near Natchez.

Emerald Mound is one of the largest Indian mounds in the United States. The mound covers about 8 acres (3 hectares) and is near Natchez, Mississippi.

Of all the structures along the Natchez Trace, the First Presbyterian Church in Port Gibson, Mississippi, symbolizes the faith and determination of the people who walked

The First Presbyterian church, in Port Gibson, Mississippi, is one of the most famous landmarks in the South.

the trail. Atop the church's spire is a golden hand, originally carved to honor the church's first pastor, Reverend Zebulin Butler. He was in the habit of punctuating his powerful sermons with "an upraised and clenched hand . . . the index finger pointing heavenward."

The golden hand may have saved Port Gibson during the American Civil War (1861–1865). On May 1, 1863, Ulysses S. Grant's Union forces marched through the town on their way to Vicksburg, Mississippi. The Union forces defeated the Confederate forces in the Battle of Port Gibson. The Union officers chose not to destroy Port Gibson, saying it was "too beautiful to burn."

Travelers on the Natchez Trace Parkway see the golden hand today. Repaired and replaced time and time again, it continues to inspire people. The golden hand transports visitors back in time to the days when the Natchez Trace linked the young but growing United States to its southwestern frontier.

GLOSSARY

Bandits on the Natchez Trace

bandit – an armed robber, usually a member of a gang

depot – a place where people store or sell supplies

dispatch – an important official government message

flatboat – a boat with a flat bottom and square ends that carries people, animals, and cargo in shallow water

ford – (noun) the place where a river or stream is crossed; (verb) to cross a river or stream

frontier – the far edge of a country, where few people live

goods – items that can be bought or sold

heyday – the time of greatest popularity, power, or success

mound – a small hill or heap of dirt

outlaw – a criminal, especially one who is running away from the law

parkway – a scenic highway

Emerald Mound, one of the largest Indian mounds in the U.S., is near Natchez, Mississippi.

pillory – a device once used for punishing people in public consisting of a wooden frame with holes in which the head and hands can be locked

port – a town that has a harbor for ships taking on or delivering cargo

stand – a place where travelers could eat and rest

territory – part of the United States that is not yet admitted as a state

trade – the business of buying and selling goods

vigilante committee – a group of volunteers who pursue outlaws

TIMELINE

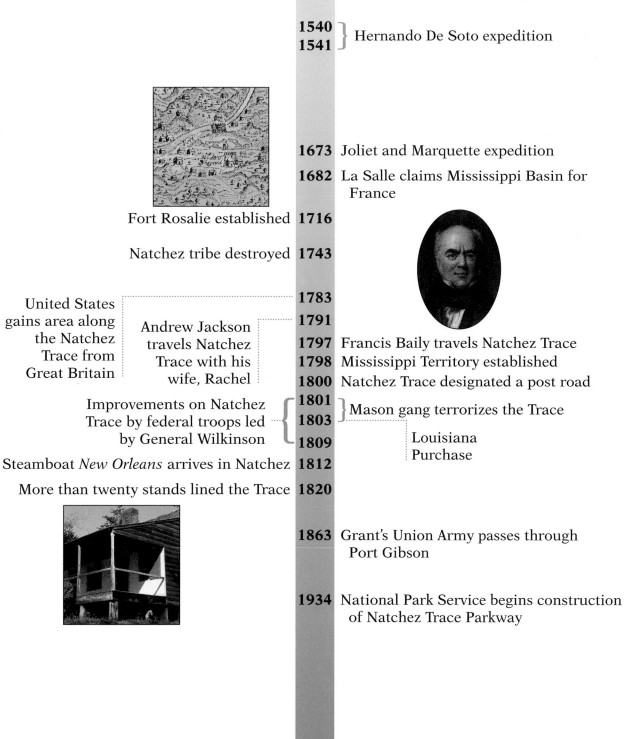

1540
1541 Hernando De Soto expedition

1673 Joliet and Marquette expedition

1682 La Salle claims Mississippi Basin for France

Fort Rosalie established **1716**

Natchez tribe destroyed **1743**

United States gains area along the Natchez Trace from Great Britain **1783**

Andrew Jackson travels Natchez Trace with his wife, Rachel **1791**

1797 Francis Baily travels Natchez Trace

1798 Mississippi Territory established

1800 Natchez Trace designated a post road

Improvements on Natchez Trace by federal troops led by General Wilkinson **1801** Mason gang terrorizes the Trace

1803

1809 Louisiana Purchase

Steamboat *New Orleans* arrives in Natchez **1812**

More than twenty stands lined the Trace **1820**

1863 Grant's Union Army passes through Port Gibson

1934 National Park Service begins construction of Natchez Trace Parkway

PHOTO CREDITS

Photographs ©: Corbis-Bettmann: 8, 31 center (Hulton-Deutsch Collection), cover, (David Muench), 5, 7 bottom, 17; Mississippi Department of Archives & History: 7 top, 23 (Special Collections Section); Mississippi Department of Economic and Community Development/Division of Tourism Development: 24; National Park Service, Natchez Trace Parkway: 14, 26, 27, 30 bottom, 31 bottom; North Wind Picture Archives: 1, 11, 13, 19, 25 (N. Carter), 6, 16, 21, 30 top, 31 top; Port Gibson-Claiborne County Chamber of Commerce: 28; Stock Montage, Inc.: 22 (The Newberry Library), 18, 20; Tennessee Tourist Development: 12. Map by TJS Design.

PICTURE IDENTIFICATIONS

Cover: Heavily wooded sections of the Natchez Trace seem dark even when the sun shines.
Page 1: Spring wildflowers bloom along the Natchez Trace. This section of the Trace is near Bear Creek, in Alabama.
Page 2: This map of the Natchez Trace shows sites mentioned in this book.

ABOUT THE AUTHORS

Charles and Linda George are former teachers who have authored more than two dozen nonfiction books for children and young adults. For Children's Press, they have written for series including Cornerstones of Freedom, Community Builders, and America the Beautiful, Second Series.

   Mr. and Mrs. George live in the mountains of New Mexico, near the small village of Cloudcroft. They enjoy traveling in their travel trailer to do research and gather ideas for new projects.

DATE			